THE DEADLY DIAMONDS

by
Laurence and Irene Swinburne

A
cpi
Book

RSVP
RAINTREE
STECK-VAUGHN
P U B L I S H E R S
The Steck-Vaughn Company

Austin, Texas

First Steck-Vaughn Edition 1992

Art and Photo Credits

Cover illustrations, Lynn Sweat.
Illustrations on pages 5, 12, and 43, New York Public Library.
Illustrations on pages 7, 8, 9, 14, 16, 22, 26, 30, 31, 33, 37, and 45, Connie Maltese.
Photo on page 42, Wide World Photos.
All photo research for this book was provided by Roberta Guerrette.
Every effort has been made to trace the ownership of all copyrighted material in this book and to obtain permission for its use.

Library of Congress Number: 77-10764

Library of Congress Cataloging in Publication Data

Swinburne, Laurence
  The deadly diamonds.

  SUMMARY: Briefly traces the history and attendant bad luck of the Regent, Pigott, Hope, and other famous diamonds.
  1. Diamonds—Juvenile literature [1. Diamonds]
I. Swinburne, Irene, joint author. II. Title.
TS753.S92   001.9'3   77-10764

ISBN 0-8172-1064-4 hardcover library binding

ISBN 0-8114-6856-9 softcover binding

16 17 18 19 20   97 96 95 94 93

Contents

Chapter 1

Alexander
and the Diamonds

The ancient Greeks had a wonderful way of telling a story. They could take a simple tale and add to it until it became a great adventure. They "shined" their stories as gems are shined. Here is one they loved to tell about their mighty warrior, Alexander the Great.

Alexander led his small, well-trained army through the huge Indian continent. His rugged Greek soldiers crashed India's borders and captured her cities. The Greeks were amazed. Never had they seen such beauty. It was like entering a land of magic. Such buildings, such temples, such cities!

"And what," Alexander asked, "are these bright stones that seemed to have the very sun trapped inside them?"

"Diamonds, Sire!" was the answer.

"Beautiful," he said, watching them twinkle as he rolled them in his hand. "Where can these diamonds be found?" Alexander asked his frightened Indian captives.

The Indians seemed nervous, as if they did not wish to give up some secret. They trembled before his piercing eyes. "In . . . a valley," one of them finally said, "but it is . . . dangerous to go there."

Alexander smiled and ordered them to lead the way to the Valley of Diamonds. These Indians might be frightened, but *he* knew no fear.

The Indians took Alexander and his soldiers to the valley. But they suddenly stopped. Alexander shouted at them, but they would not go one step further. "Beware, Alexander, of the thousands of snakes crawling in the valley," they said. "They were put there by our gods to protect the diamonds. They are small, but they are the most deadly snakes known. They only have

"Beautiful! Where can these diamonds be found?"

to crawl near to you, stare in your face, and you will fall down dead!"

Alexander thought for a few minutes. The Indians were truly afraid. Maybe what they were saying was true. On the other hand, the diamonds were so beautiful. If only he had a plan. Suddenly he turned and spoke to his soldiers. "You who have hand mirrors, go forward with me!"

Before the horrified eyes of the Indians, Alexander walked boldly into the valley, holding a mirror in front of him. The snakes hissed and spat. Slowly, they crawled toward him and his men. The Indians thought Alexander would

Alexander walked boldly into the valley, holding a mirror
in front of him.

surely be killed. But when the vile snakes saw
their own faces in the mirrors, it was they who
met death. Soon the whole valley was covered
with the bodies of dead snakes.

In the center of the valley was a deep pit.
More snakes twisted at its dark bottom. But in
this pit there were also hundreds of sparkling
diamonds. How could he reach the stones with
those snakes in there?

Alexander knew the mirror trick would not
work again. His men couldn't go down on ropes
and still hold their mirrors correctly. Then, he
thought of another plan.

"Kill a few sheep," he ordered. "Make sure that each has a thick coat of fleece."

The dead sheep were thrown into the pit. As they landed, diamonds became twisted in their thick and curly coats.

Drawn by the smell of death, the vultures swooped down from the sky. They flew into the pit and grabbed the dead sheep in their sharp claws. Then the huge birds rose into the air.

Alexander pointed. "Shoot them!"

No sooner had he spoken than a rain of Greek arrows shot upward into the sky. Down fell the vultures. From the fleeces of the dead sheep, Alexander calmly plucked the brilliant diamonds.

Wars have been fought over them. Thieves have risked their lives just to steal them. Certain ones have a value that is unbelievable—people pay thousands, even millions of dollars to buy them.

What are they? *Diamonds*—beautiful, shining stones from the earth. Yet, for all their beauty, for all their value, these brilliant, sun-filled gems have often brought people misery.

This book is all about diamonds. Every story deals with the wonder and excitement of the precious stones. And every story tells of the misfortunes that befell people who came under the spell of the diamond.

Are these stories of the "deadly diamonds" just mixtures of coincidence and superstition? Some think so. Others believe diamonds can be as unlucky as they are beautiful. You will have to judge for yourself!

Chapter

2

The Case of the Regent Diamond

Ancient India was the home of the diamond. For 2,000 years almost all diamonds came from this land.

It was a long trip for Europeans to reach India—filled with danger and risk. Jean Baptiste Tavernier, a Frenchman, risked his life many times making the trip to India. The diamonds he brought back sold for very high prices, and his dangerous travel had made him rich. The King of France was one of his best customers. The King was so pleased with Tavernier's diamonds

Jean Baptiste Tavernier was a French diamond merchant at the time of Louis XIV.

that he made him a baron. Others were not so fond of diamonds as the King, however.

Some diamonds were said to have an evil buried within them. Their owners appeared to be followed by bad luck from the time they got them, until they were rid of them. There were many such tales. Take the case of the *Regent Diamond*. Would *you* like to own it?

No one knows the name of the Indian miner who first found the Regent stone in 1701. We do know that he was a badly paid, hungry man who worked 12 hours a day, *every day* of the week. He was a mining slave. That's the way all Indian miners—men, women, and small children— were treated.

The lucky miner probably couldn't believe his eyes when he found the bright, clear rock. Here was a diamond that would surely bring him great riches. But how was he to get it out of the mine? Workers were carefully searched at the end of each day.

For what this diamond was worth, this miner would try *anything*. Hiding himself, he slashed his leg with a sharp knife. It must have hurt him very badly, but the hope of escaping

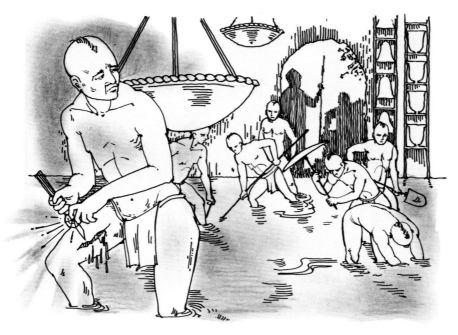

Hiding himself, he slashed his leg with a sharp knife.
He then pushed the diamond into the wound and wrapped
a rag around his leg.

with the diamond kept him from fainting. He pushed the rough diamond into the wound and wrapped a rag around his leg.

A soldier searched him as usual when he came out of the mine. "What's wrong with your leg?" the soldier asked.

"I cut it badly," the miner said, shaking in fear.

14

The soldier waved him on. Miners were always getting hurt down there. What difference did it make? They never lived long, anyway.

The miner limped to the port of Madras. He looked over the ships in the bay and finally chose one. It was not the best of ships and it wasn't very clean. But it was an English ship and the miner thought that traders from England would offer the best deal.

The English captain knew much about diamonds. He studied the miner's gem carefully. The captain frowned to hide his true feelings, but he could hardly still his shaking hands. This was the largest diamond he had ever seen.

"It's a fair stone, lad," he said as he handed it back. "But I don't have any money with me. I have it hidden in the city—*Delhi*. Know where that is?"

The miner was annoyed. Did the Englishman think he was stupid? He nodded. "It's up north."

"That's right. Well, you've come just in time. We're ready to sail."

Once the land was out of sight, the captain said, "Let's see that rock again. I think there's something wrong with it."

"No, no." The miner shook his head. "It's a real diamond. Here, see for yourself."

As soon as the diamond was in the captain's hand, he nodded his head to two sailors standing nearby. One hit the Indian on the head with a club. Before the miner had fallen to the deck,

The poor Indian miner was outsmarted by the English captain.

the other sailor threw him overboard. The captain hardly heard the splash. He stared at the diamond with greedy eyes. "What luck! I'm a rich man," he thought to himself.

Rich. Yes, he was rich for a while. But he wasn't so lucky. The cruel captain sold the stone to a jeweler named Jamchaud for 1,000 pounds —then worth about $6,000. But the sea captain drank and gambled the money away in a very short time. Either because he knew he would never see that much cash again, or because the ghost of the Indian miner haunted him, he hanged himself.

What about Jamchaud? This might have been the best diamond he had ever bought for so little money. But he did not have an easy time selling such a huge diamond. People who looked at it were fascinated, but they drew away. It certainly was beautiful, all right. There was just something about it, something they couldn't put their fingers on, something . . . *wrong.*

Only one person showed interest in the diamond. His name was Thomas Pitt. He was the young English governor of Madras, but he wasn't very rich. All he could pay was 20,400 pounds. Fearing that he would never find a better buyer, Jamchaud took Pitt's offer.

Pitt's life changed soon after his "lucky" purchase. He had always been a happy-go-lucky fellow. Now, overnight, he had become a suspicious man who never went to parties and hardly ever talked. He slept with the diamond under his pillow and kept a loaded pistol by his bed. He lived with the fear of being murdered by robbers. People began to whisper that perhaps the governor himself had stolen the gem.

When Pitt returned to England a few years later, an ugly story of his "stolen" jewel followed him. People avoided him, and he avoided people. He blamed the valuable diamond for his unhappiness. It was too big to keep at home and it was too big to sell!

Finally, Pitt was able to sell the diamond to the French royal family for a whopping 135,000 pounds!

For the first time in many years, Thomas Pitt thought he could be happy. The diamond that had brought him so much misery and had almost driven him crazy was finally gone. Yet he was to find no peace. The story that he had really stolen the gem followed him everywhere. That story may even have caused his unexpected and untimely death.

The stone's evil spell slept for 75 years. But it awoke when the French Revolution began. King Louis XVI was thrown into prison by the angry people of France. He was finally beheaded.

The French government put the Regent Diamond into the Louvre Museum. It's been there for almost 100 years. The strange thing is —no one seems to want to steal it.

Chapter

3

The Case of the Pigott Diamond

After Thomas Pitt, Lord George Pigott, too, was the English governor of the Indian port of Madras. Like Pitt, he owned a large diamond. But Pigott's diamond was a gift from an Indian nobleman.

When Pigott retired, he returned to England. There, he cheated some people out of their money and was thrown into prison. He died a prisoner, leaving his family with hardly a cent, but with one large, beautiful diamond. The Pigott family tried to figure out how to sell it.

But how could they sell it? They wouldn't trust the jewelers to tell them the true value of the gem. Instead, they formed a lottery, the diamond being the only prize. The winner of the lottery then sold the diamond to a jeweler. A short time later it was bought by Ali Pasha, a Turkish nobleman.

In those days, just before the American Revolution, Turkey ruled Albania where Ali Pasha was governor. Ali Pasha was a brutal man. He could order a thousand people tortured and killed without having a moment's guilt.

He could look calmly upon the starving Albanians. He was a man with little sympathy. These poor people were taxed so heavily, they hardly had clothes to wear. Ali Pasha was blind to their suffering.

But Ali Pasha did have his softer side. There were two things he loved. One was the Pigott diamond. He wore it in his turban every day. At night he would place the glittering stone by his bed, where he would always be close to it.

His other love was his wife, Vasilikee. She was very different from him. She was beautiful, and he was ugly. She was young and he was

At night Ali Pasha would place the glittering stone by his bed.

middle-aged. She was gentle and kind, while he was hard and cruel.

Everyone who knew them saw that Ali Pasha's love was not returned by Vasilikee. When he came near, she drew back, in terror. When he touched her, she would faint. She had never wanted to marry him, but Ali Pasha had threatened her father. The cruel governor would have had the man's entire family burned to death if Vasilikee had not wed him. What was her poor father to do? The marriage of his daughter, even to such a monster, was better than the killing of his whole family.

One day though, Ali Pasha's luck turned. His greed had made the Turkish sultan angry. The sultan didn't care about the way his governor treated the people of Albania. No, Ali Pasha had done a more terrible thing in the eyes of the sultan. As governor, he had kept much of the tax money he collected instead of sending it to the sultan.

A company of Turkish soldiers appeared at Ali Pasha's castle. The captain bowed low, but his eyes showed no respect. "His Royal Highness, our great sultan, has asked for you," the captain said. "He feels he can no longer do without your company. He wishes to reward the great services you have given him as ruler of Albania."

Now Ali Pasha may have been cruel, but he wasn't stupid. He knew very well what lay behind the smooth words. He was being politely *arrested*. He would be taken back to the Turkish capital of Istanbul and thrown into prison . . . if he was lucky. Maybe he could escape to France. Perhaps there was still time.

Suddenly, Ali Pasha pointed a bony finger at the Turkish captain. "These people are imposters," he screamed at his guards. "They have come here to rob us! To the dungeons with them!"

But Ali Pasha's guards knew better. These newcomers were not fakes. Fight the sultan's soldiers? Only fools would do that! The guards did not move.

Ali Pasha may have been wise, but his wisdom wasn't helping him at the moment. Well, Ali Pasha was no coward. He drew his sword and tried to cut his way out. The one-sided battle was over in a few minutes. Ali Pasha lay in a pool of his own blood. "I am dying," he croaked to the captain. "I have only two wishes, very simple ones. You cannot deny a dying man his two wishes."

"I promise by Allah that if your wishes will bring no harm to my master, the sultan, nor make him angry, I will do as you ask."

The governor gave a cheerless laugh. "Oh, it won't hurt him at all. I—" His face twisted in pain and he could barely get the words out. "I want my two greatest treasures destroyed!"

The captain shrugged his shoulders. "A strange wish. But I have given my word. What are these treasures?"

"My wife, Vasilikee, and the diamond on my turban!"

The soldier looked at the dying man with disgust. "You want me to kill someone who is not my enemy?"

"Two beautiful things and mine alone," murmured Ali Pasha. "Their loss will not harm the sultan. You promised, soldier, you promised by Allah!"

Vasilikee was brought into the room, shaking with fear. "You know your husband's order —what he wants me to do to you?" asked the captain.

She hung her head. "He had told me many times he would have me killed at his death."

"And the shame of this is I have given my word to do this terrible deed." He turned again to Ali Pasha. "Well, which would you have destroyed first?"

The governor opened his mouth to speak, then closed it. He couldn't make up his mind. He looked at the diamond which had been placed on the floor, then at Vasilikee, then at the diamond again. A few moments of silence passed.

Ali Pasha pointed to the diamond. "First the jewel."

The captain smashed at the gem again and again with the flat of his sword. He did not stop until the floor glittered with diamond dust. With each blow, Ali Pasha groaned. "Enough?" asked the soldier in a cold voice.

But Ali Pasha did not answer. The captain leaned down and felt for a heartbeat. There was

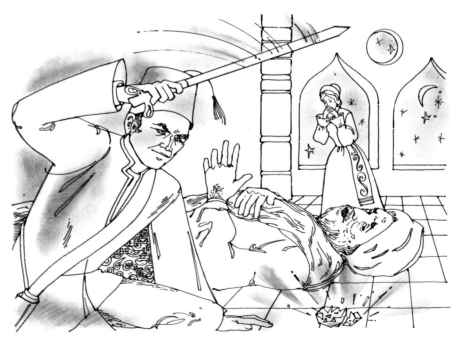

The captain smashed at the gem again and again with the flat of his sword.

none. Ali Pasha was dead. When the captain rose, he was smiling!

"Vasilikee," he said, "you are lucky that Ali Pasha loved the diamond a bit more than you. If he had loved you more, you would be dead. As it is, he is dead, and I no longer feel I have to carry out his last wish. You are free to go."

Before the captain left, he took one last look at the twisted body on the floor. "Ah, governor, you were so wrong in your choice. A human being is a human being, but a diamond is only a stone!"

The Queen's Necklace Caper

It was the world's finest necklace. At least, that's what everyone who saw it thought. Its 500 sparkling diamonds could blind a person. Like Ali Pasha's diamond, it is gone forever. It disappeared because of a young queen, a foolish cardinal, and a group of clever robbers.

When King Louis XV of France was an old man, he sent for Boehmer and Bassange, the most skilled jewelers in the country.

"I want to give a gift to a lady," he told them. "It must be something wonderful."

"What did you have in mind, your majesty?" asked Boehmer. "An emerald ring? A ruby bracelet? A large diamond?"

"Diamonds! That's more like it. But not just one! A *necklace* of diamonds—that's the idea. One that will outshine all others."

The jewelers drew plans and showed them to the ruler. The necklace they planned had 500 diamonds.

The king held the plans up to the light. "Simply beautiful," he said. "But the diamonds must be perfect, every one of them. Do you hear?"

"Every one?" gasped Bassange. "But to find so many perfect stones would take a great deal of time and money."

"Money and time, what are they when you are making a great work of art? Go ahead, gentlemen. You have my backing."

It took the jewelers two years to find all the stones. They were excited at the job they had done. But they were also sad for they knew they would never make anything for the rest of their lives that would be better than this necklace.

The jewelers, Boehmer and Bassange, created "the world's finest necklace" for Louis XV.

But King Louis XV died before he could see this jeweled masterpiece. At first the jewelers were not bothered by his death. After all, the old king had ordered the necklace. Wouldn't the new king pay for it?

As it turned out, the next king, Louis XVI, was a young man and not very sure of himself. He was never able to take a strong stand in all his life. He liked the necklace, but his wife, Marie Antoinette, refused to have it purchased. For one thing, she had already spent a small fortune on diamonds. Also, the French were then involved in the American Revolution. That took a great deal of money!

Marie Antoinette cared nothing about the problems of the jewelers. They cried at her feet, but she told them coldly, "I won't buy it even if you drown in your tears."

As you have guessed, Marie Antoinette is the "young queen" of our story. Now, enter the robbers. Their plan was the work of a poor nobleman, Count Mark Antony de la Motte, and his wife, Jeanne, who was called "La Valois."

Marie Antoinette told the jewelers coldly, "I won't buy it even if you drown in your tears."

Their careful plan included a magician, an actress, and a forger. Their victim was to be not the Queen, but the very rich and very foolish Cardinal de Rohan.

When Marie Antoinette was very young, the cardinal said some nasty things about her. She had neither forgotten, nor forgiven, him. She had been Queen for four years. In all that time, Marie Antoinette never said one word to the cardinal.

The cardinal had tried many times to apologize to the Queen. But the more he tried, the more she hated him. De Rohan felt this very deeply. If only, he thought, there were some way to become her friend.

La Valois managed to meet the cardinal. She blinked her wide, innocent-looking eyes and told him that she was very close to the Queen. In fact, if the cardinal would write another apology, she herself would deliver it. Also, she would try her best to talk the Queen into "letting bygones be bygones."

De Rohan was ready to believe anything. He was taken in by La Valois' innocence and beauty. He decided to write the letter of apology. A few days later, La Valois returned. Her bright smile told him she had good news.

"The Queen wishes to meet with you. It must be done in secret, though, you understand. Meet her at midnight in the palace gardens."

The cardinal was there a half hour early. La Valois was waiting for him. "Come," she whispered, "but be very quiet." Taking his hand, she led him to a dark part of the gardens. She left him there and he spent a few minutes, waiting.

La Valois took the cardinal's hand and led him to a dark part of the gardens.

Then a dark figure appeared from nowhere. "Cardinal de Rohan?" said a cold voice.

He fell to his knees and kissed her hand. "Forgive me, Your Highness, forgive me," he said, tears in his eyes.

"Rise, rise," said the dark figure impatiently. "The past is forgotten."

"Let me prove my loyalty," said de Rohan. "Let me be of service to you in any way you wish."

"There are some things I may want you to do," said the woman. "Let me think about it. For the time being, you are not to tell anyone about this meeting. There are reasons for this I cannot go into now. I must go, but you will hear from me through Jeanne La Valois."

She gave him a box and slipped into the darkness. A moment later, La Valois appeared and guided him out of the royal gardens.

When he returned to his home, de Rohan opened the box. He was delighted to find a rose and a picture of Marie Antoinette. She had forgiven him, he was sure.

He would not have been so happy if he could have seen La Valois at that moment. That lady was handing money to a woman who looked like the Queen . . . especially in the dark.

"You did your job well," said La Valois.

The woman smiled as she looked at the money. "This is more than I get for a whole month of acting on the stage." The first part of the plan had been completed. But there was much more to come. La Valois visited the cardinal a few days later.

She told the cardinal that the Queen wanted the Louis XV necklace. "She cannot buy it herself right now, but in two years she will have the money and will pay you then. She has signed a letter, stating this." La Valois handed him a paper.

He read it carefully. Yes, it was just as La Valois said. And that was certainly the Queen's signature. He had seen it many times. But the great diamond necklace—what a price to pay for friendship!

"If your excellency doesn't wish to get back in the Queen's good graces or doesn't have that much money. . ."

He waved his hand. "No, no, it's not that. But I must think about it. I'll let you know in a few days."

That evening Cardinal de Rohan invited Count de Cagliostro to dinner. Cagliostro was no more a count than the woman in the palace garden was a real queen. He was an Italian magician who told strange stories in a very convincing way.

The cardinal told the fake count what had happened. "What do you think, my friend? What should I do?"

"I believe, great Cardinal, that you are wise to be careful in this matter. However, I shall try to find out the truth for you."

Cagliostro's eyes fluttered, closed, and he became lost in a "trance." He began talking in a strange, ghostly voice: "My mind is leaving my body. It floats from here and is now traveling over the city of Paris. I am at the Palace of Versailles. I am now entering the bedroom of the Queen. My mind is drawing out thoughts from the Queen's brain. She is thinking . . . she is thinking . . . about a beautiful necklace. She is hoping that Cardinal de Rohan, whom she

Cagliostro's eyes fluttered, closed, and he became
lost in a "trance."

now thinks of as her friend, will be able to get
this beautiful jewelry for her. She . . . she. . ."

That was all. Cagliostro's head fell onto his
chest. It was five minutes before he opened his
eyes and groaned. "I have such a headache.
These mind journeys are so painful. What did I
say, for I remember nothing of these spells?"

"You have discovered that La Valois is telling the truth," shouted the delighted, but simple, cardinal. "That's all I had to know. The
Queen will *have* her necklace."

A short time later, Cagliostro was repeating these words to La Valois and her husband. "Remember that my share is one-third," said the magician. The crooks didn't care. The price was small enough. There would be plenty left over for them to live in comfort.

They staged the switching of the diamond necklace as if they were directing a play. The cardinal bought the jewelry from Boehmer and Bassange. Soon after, La Valois brought a letter, supposedly from the Queen. Would her good friend, the great Cardinal de Rohan, be so kind as to bring the necklace to the house of Count de la Motte? The Queen wished to wear the necklace at a party the next evening.

Later that day, de Rohan arrived at the Motte's. There, a man, dressed in royal uniform, was waiting. "I have been ordered here, Your Excellency, to pick up something for the Queen."

The cardinal suspected nothing. He took a box from his robe and handed it to the man. The "messenger" (who was really the forger of the contract and the letter) bowed and left.

That night the thieves took apart the neck-lace with a knife. They would have liked to sell the whole necklace to one buyer. They knew, however, they could not do what Boehmer and Bassange had tried to do and failed.

The diamonds were sold, one by one. The money they made should have allowed them to live in ease for the rest of their lives. But they did not have the willpower to control them-selves. They began to spend money wildly. People wondered where the Mottes had found this flood of cash.

When the robbery story was known, Count Mark Antony de la Motte was sentenced to be branded with hot irons and to work at hard labor in prison for the rest of his life. Luckily for the count, he was in England at the time. He had gone there to sell more of the diamonds. He decided to stay there, rather than return for his punishment.

La Valois, like her husband, was given a life sentence. Unluckily for her, she had not gone on her husband's business trip with him. She was branded and thrown into prison. Clever woman that she was, however, she managed to escape after a year. She then made her way to England where she finally did join her husband.

Cagliostro was found innocent. After all, who would put an old magician in a jail cell?

That's about the end of the Queen's Necklace Caper, except, of course, for Cardinal de Rohan. As for him, poor fellow, he never was forgiven by the Queen. She despised him all the more for daring to believe that she would select *him* to buy *her* a necklace of diamonds.

Oh, you may be wondering why a story that ends this happily is in a book that deals with the curse of the "deadly diamonds." As you remember, King Louis XVI was beheaded at the guillotine on January 21, 1793. Shortly after, his wife, Marie Antoinette, lost her head to the same blade.

The Deadly Hope Diamond

Any diamond by the name of Hope sounds like it might bring good luck. The Hope Diamond, however, was far from a good-luck charm. Its name comes from a family that once owned it . . . and later wished it hadn't!

Remember Jean Baptiste Tavernier, the Frenchman of the 1600s? He was the one who sold diamonds from India to the French king.

One striking gem Tavernier brought back was bluish—an unusual color for a diamond.

The Hope Diamond was called "The Blue Diamond of the Crown" by King Louis XIV.

King Louis XIV loved it and named it "The Blue Diamond of the Crown."

There was a story going around France that this stone was once the right eye of a statue of the Indian god, Rama-Sita. It was even hinted that Tavernier *stole* the diamond. Since Rama-Sita was a vengeful god, he sent a curse after it. After all, who likes to have his eye stolen?

At any rate, when Louis XIV died of small-pox, the diamond was blamed. The curse of the diamond skipped over the next king. But then, as we know, Louis XVI and his wife had their heads cut off.

The Indian god, Rama-Sita.

Sometime during the French Revolution, the "Blue Diamond" was robbed along with the "Regent Diamond." Forty years later, an English banker, Henry Philip Hope, bought a much smaller blue diamond. It was later learned that the Blue Diamond of Louis XVI had been cut into three diamonds. One of these was the one Mr. Hope bought and it came to be called the *Hope Diamond.*

Henry Hope passed through life without too much bad luck. So did the diamond's next owner, his nephew. The god Rama-Sita must have been sleeping. However, soon after the nephew's grandson got the diamond, his wife ran off and he lost all his money.

An actress wore it once—*her boyfriend later murdered her. A rich Greek bought it—he and his whole family fell off a cliff. The Sultan of Turkey no sooner bought the diamond than a revolution broke out.*

Then the Hope Diamond passed on to the McLean family of the United States. Mrs. McLean fell in love with the sparkling blue stone. She met with no harm herself, but many around her suffered the worst of luck. Her husband's last years were spent in a mental hospital.

Her daughter took her own life, and her son was killed in an automobile accident.

Mrs. McLean never believed in the curse of Rama-Sita. During World War II, she took the precious stone to military hospitals. There it was handled by hundreds of wounded soldiers and sailors.

The Bad Luck of the Hope Diamond
An actress was murdered by her boyfriend.
A rich Greek fell off a cliff with his family.
The Sultan of Turkey faced a revolution.

When she died, the Hope Diamond was bought by Harry Winston, a New York jeweler. He decided to give it to the Smithsonian Institution in Washington, D.C. But how was he to get it there safely? He knew some people would do anything to get their hands on it. Finally, he let "Uncle Sam" carry it. Harry Winston mailed the stone!

The diamond arrived at that famous Washington museum, safe and sound. If you get a chance to look at it at the Smithsonian some day, just think of the bad times so many of the blue stone's owners suffered . . . and then decide if *you* would like to own it.